Managing Editor
Ina Massler Levin, M.A.

Editor
Eric Migliaccio

Contributing Editor
Sarah Smith

Creative Director
Karen J. Goldfluss, M.S. Ed.

Cover Design
Tony Carrillo / Marilyn Goldberg

Teacher Created Resources
12621 Western Avenue
Garden Grove, CA 92841
www.teachercreated.com

ISBN: 978-1-4206-5939-9

©2007 Teacher Created Resources
Reprinted, 2024 (PO605505)
Made in U.S.A.

The material in this book is intended for individual use only. No part of this publication may be transmitted, reproduced, stored, or recorded in any form without written permission from the publisher.

This book belongs to

_____

Ready·Set·Learn

Get Ready to Learn!

Get ready, get set, and go! Boost your child's learning with this exciting series of books. Geared to help children practice and master many needed skills, the *Ready·Set·Learn* books are bursting with 64 pages of learning fun. Use these books for...

 enrichment  skills reinforcement  extra practice

With their smaller size, the *Ready·Set·Learn* books fit easily in children's hands, backpacks, and book bags. All your child needs to get started are pencils, crayons, and colored pencils.

A full sheet of colorful stickers is included. Use these stickers for...

- decorating pages
- rewarding outstanding effort
- keeping track of completed pages

Celebrate your child's progress by using these stickers on the reward chart located on the inside cover. The blue-ribbon sticker fits perfectly on the certificate on page 64.

With *Ready·Set·Learn* and a little encouragement, your child will be on the fast track to learning fun!

Colorful Addition

Directions: Count the pictures to find the sum.

1.  +  = _____ kittens

2. +  = _____ pigs

3.  + = _____ pencils

4.  + = _____ books

5. Mary had eleven pieces of candy. Her sister, Sarah, gave her three more pieces of candy. How many total pieces of candy did Mary have?

    Draw your answer, then write the equation and the sum.

_____ + _____ = _____

Add to Ten

Directions: Each number pair should equal 10. Write the missing numbers.

1. 8 + ____ = 10

2. 7 + ____ = 10

3. 9 + ____ = 10

4. 10 + ____ = 10

5. 6 + ____ = 10

6. 4 + ____ = 10

7. 2 + ____ = 10

8. 5 + ____ = 10

9. 1 + ____ = 10

Busy Bee Addition

Directions: Help the bee find the right flower. Solve the problems. Draw a line from the bee to the flower with the sum of 11. Color the picture.

1. 2 + 6 = __
2. 9 + 1 = __
3. 4 + 10 = __
4. 8 + 3 = __
5. 4 + 8 = __
6. 5 + 7 = __

Four Frolicking Frogs

Directions: Each number pair should equal 5. Write the missing numbers. Then follow the directions.

- Use a green crayon to color the frog that had the missing number 0.
- Use a red crayon to color the frog that had the missing number 4.
- Use a purple crayon to color the frog that had the missing number 3.
- Use an orange crayon to color the frog that had the missing number 2.

1.
   3 + ___ = 5

2.
   5 + ___ = 5

3. 1 + ___ = 5

4. 2 + ___ = 5

Add Them Up

Directions: Add the numbers.

1. 5 + 11

2. 14 + 0

3. 13 + 1

4. 11 + 4

5. 10 + 2

6. 3 + 12

7. 7 + 10

8. 5 + 13

9. 7 + 9

10. 6 + 9

11. 15 + 3

12. 14 + 3

Directions: Add the numbers. Write the answer on the line.

13. 1 + 1 + 1 = ____

14. 5 + 1 + 4 = ____

15. 1 + 2 + 3 = ____

16. 2 + 4 + 6 = ____

Back-and-Forth Addition

Directions: Write the answer to each addition problem.

1.
```
  12
+  6
----
```

2.
```
   6
+ 12
----
```

3.
```
   9
+  8
----
```

4.
```
   8
+  9
----
```

5.
```
  13
+  1
----
```

6.
```
   1
+ 13
----
```

7.
```
  10
+  5
----
```

8.
```
   5
+ 10
----
```

Directions: Complete the math problem for each of the word problems.

9. Janie has 7 pigs. She buys 5 more pigs. How many pigs does Janie have now?

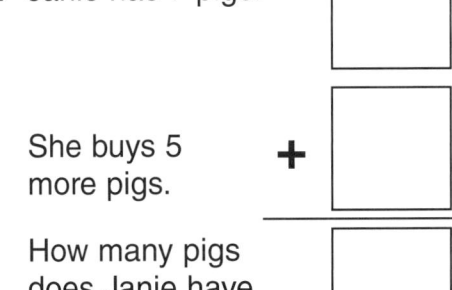

10. Bill gathered 5 eggs. Then he gathered 7 more eggs. How many eggs does Bill have now?

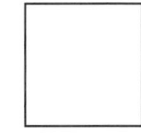

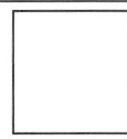

Double Take

Directions: Knowing the sum of doubles helps you add faster.

Directions: Solve these problems.

1. 5 + 5 =
2. 7 + 7 =
3. 9 + 9 =
4. 2 + 2 =
5. 6 + 6 =

6. 3 + 3 =
7. 1 + 1 =
8. 4 + 4 =
9. 8 + 8 =
10. 10 + 10 =

Directions: Read the problem. Write it below. Find the sum.

11. Sarah has five red balloons. Her friend Andre has five blue balloons. How many balloons do they have in all? (Write the number sentence and the answer.)

 + =

Practice Makes Perfect

Directions: Add the numbers to find the sum.

1. 7 + 8 = ☐

2. 12 + 2 = ☐

3. 1 + 8 = ☐

4. 3 + 3 = ☐

5. 7 + 6 = ☐

6. 9 + 5 = ☐

7. 3
    7
  + 5
  ___

8. 6
    2
  + 7
  ___

Directions: Find the missing number.

9. 9 + ☐ = 18

10. 7 + ☐ = 10

11. 1 + ☐ = 3

12. 12 + ☐ = 16

Adding Doubles + 1

Ready·Set·Learn

Directions: Look at each pair of number facts. The first addition problem uses doubles (2 of the same number). The second addition problem uses numbers that are "neighbors" (a double + 1 more). Solve each addition problem.

1. 1 + 1 2. 1 + 2	3. 8 + 8 4. 8 + 9	5. 7 + 7 6. 7 + 8
7. 5 + 5 8. 5 + 6	9. 3 + 3 10. 3 + 4	11. 9 + 9 12. 9 + 10
13. 4 + 4 14. 4 + 5	15. 2 + 2 16. 2 + 3	17. 6 + 6 18. 6 + 7

Adding Three Numbers

Directions: When adding three numbers, add the first two numbers together. Write that answer in the box and add the third number by "counting on." Write the final answer below the line. The first one has been done for you.

1. 3
    6 > [9]
    + 8
    ———
    17

2. 9
    3 > ☐
    + 6

3. 5
    5 > ☐
    + 5

4. 3
    5 > ☐
    + 7

5. 4
    2 > ☐
    + 9

6. 7
    0 > ☐
    + 1

7. 5
    6 > ☐
    + 5

8. 5
    3 > ☐
    + 4

9. 8
    6 > ☐
    + 3

Directions: Write the missing numbers.

10. 5
     6
    +☐
    ———
    14

11. 4
     4
    +☐
    ———
    12

12. 7
     3
    +☐
    ———
    10

©Teacher Created Resources · #5939 Addition

Three's the Number

Directions: Can you add up the numbers on each can? Write the answers on the top of each can. The first one has been done for you.

Row 1

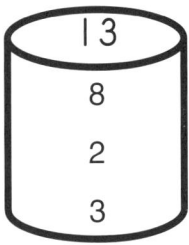 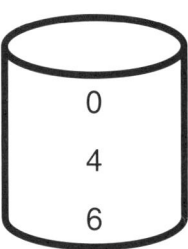 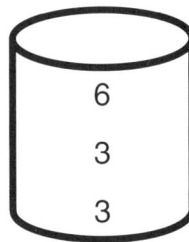 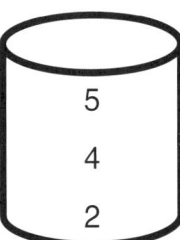

Row 2

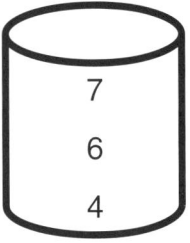 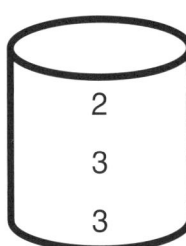 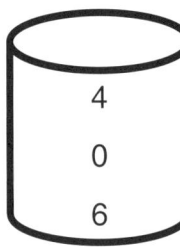 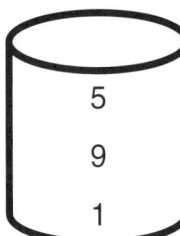

Row 3

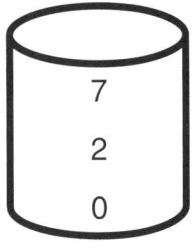 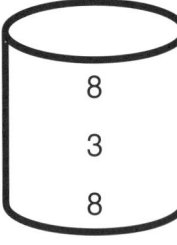 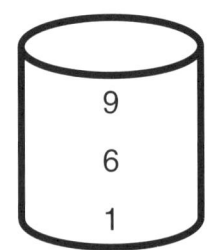 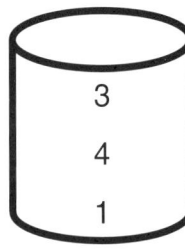

Skyscraper Math

Directions: Skyscrapers stand very tall. Add the numbers on each one. Start by adding the top two numbers together and the bottom two numbers together. Then add the sums of each of those pairs to each other.

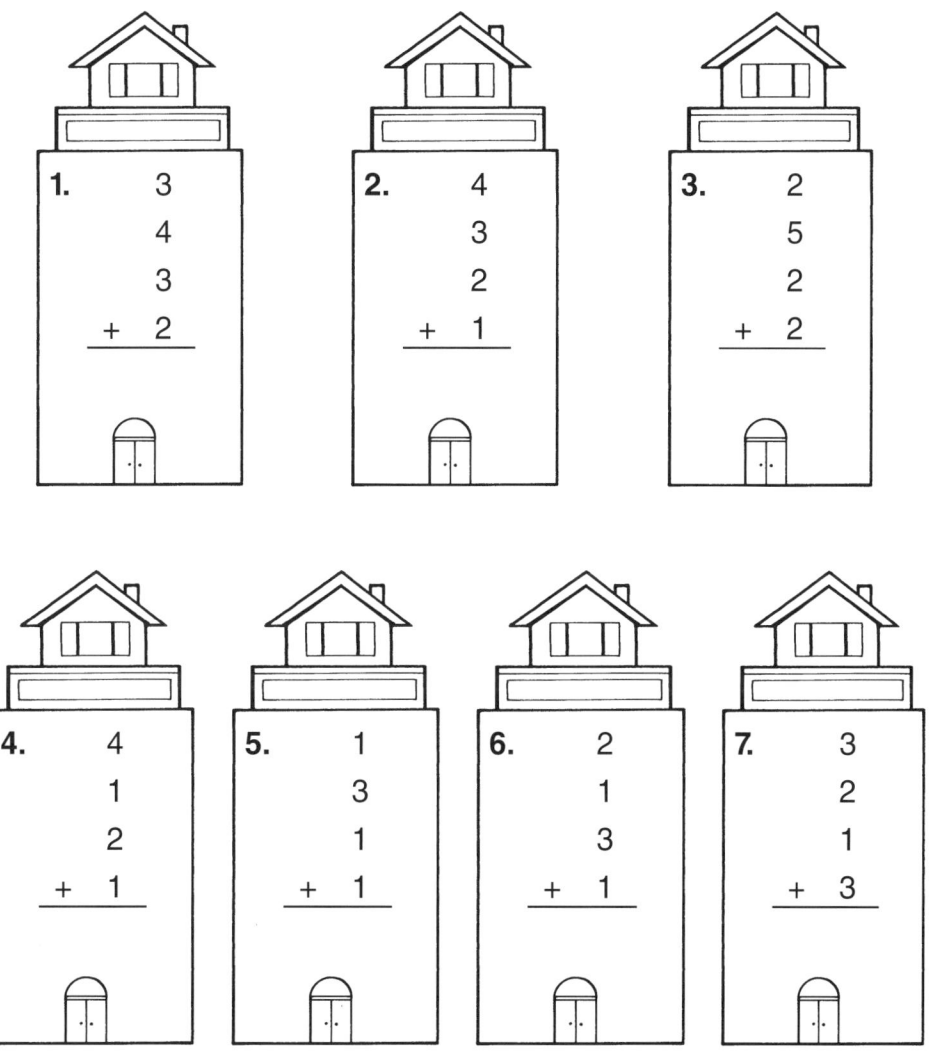

1. 3, 4, 3, + 2
2. 4, 3, 2, + 1
3. 2, 5, 2, + 2
4. 4, 1, 2, + 1
5. 1, 3, 1, + 1
6. 2, 1, 3, + 1
7. 3, 2, 1, + 3

Adding Multiple Digits

Directions: Solve each problem.

1. $\begin{array}{r} 3 \\ 4 \\ 3 \\ +2 \\ \hline \end{array}$

2. $\begin{array}{r} 2 \\ 1 \\ 3 \\ +1 \\ \hline \end{array}$

3. $\begin{array}{r} 7 \\ 2 \\ 3 \\ 1 \\ +1 \\ \hline \end{array}$

4. $\begin{array}{r} 4 \\ 3 \\ 2 \\ +1 \\ \hline \end{array}$

5. $\begin{array}{r} 3 \\ 2 \\ 1 \\ +3 \\ \hline \end{array}$

6. $\begin{array}{r} 3 \\ 5 \\ +1 \\ \hline \end{array}$

7. $\begin{array}{r} 2 \\ 5 \\ 2 \\ +2 \\ \hline \end{array}$

8. $\begin{array}{r} 2 \\ 4 \\ +2 \\ \hline \end{array}$

9. $\begin{array}{r} 6 \\ 2 \\ +3 \\ \hline \end{array}$

10. $\begin{array}{r} 4 \\ 1 \\ 2 \\ +1 \\ \hline \end{array}$

11. $\begin{array}{r} 7 \\ 2 \\ +1 \\ \hline \end{array}$

12. $\begin{array}{r} 9 \\ 2 \\ 1 \\ +1 \\ \hline \end{array}$

Money Addition

Directions: Use the prices in the box to write addition problems below. Find the sums.

1. ![doll] + ![book] =

    ___ + ___ = ___

2. ![doll] + ![yo-yo] =

    ___ + ___ = ___

3. ![bear] + ![car] =

    ___ + ___ = ___

4. ![book] + ![top] + ![car] =

    ___ + ___ + ___ = ___

5. ![puzzle] + ![doll] =

    ___ + ___ = ___

6. ![bear] + ![book] =

    ___ + ___ = ___

Word Problems

Directions: Read each word problem. Write the math problem and the answer.

1. Cheryl has 3 goldfish, 4 yellow fish, and 6 green fish. How many fish does Cheryl have in all?

   ```
     3
     4
   + 6
   ---
    13
   ```

   Cheryl has __13__ fish in all.

2. Marcus made a headband. He used 7 green feathers, 8 blue feathers, and 1 red feather. How many feathers did Marcus use in all?

   Marcus used _____ feathers in all.

3. Jasmine used beads to make a necklace. She used 6 brown beads, 5 pink beads, and 9 black beads. How many beads did Jasmine use in all?

   Jasmine used _____ beads in all.

4. Angelo likes to play marbles. He has 3 that are cat eyes, 5 that are swirled, and 6 that are solid blue. How many marbles does Angelo have in all?

   Angelo has _____ marbles in all.

Adding Two-Digit Numbers

Directions: When adding two-digit numbers, remember to always start on the ones side first.

1. tens | ones
   2 | 0
  +4 | 6

2. tens | ones
   7 | 0
  +2 | 9

3. tens | ones
   3 | 0
  +3 | 0

4. tens | ones
   3 | 7
  +5 | 0

5. tens | ones
   2 | 6
  +3 | 2

6. tens | ones
   7 | 3
  +2 | 5

7. tens | ones
   5 | 1
  +4 | 1

8. tens | ones
   1 | 8
  +3 | 1

9. tens | ones
   4 | 5
  +4 | 1

10. tens | ones
    7 | 6
   +1 | 2

11. tens | ones
    1 | 6
   +2 | 2

12. tens | ones
    4 | 0
   +4 | 9

13. Write the answers to each problem in order from smallest to greatest.

____, ____, ____, ____, ____, ____, ____, ____, ____, ____, ____, ____

Addition Circles

Directions: Find the sum of the numbers in each circle.

1. 21 + 12

2. 10 + 19

3. 40 + 24

4. 16 + 13

5. 21 + 13

6. 52 + 10

7. 32 + 11

8. 31 + 22

9. 41 + 18

Ready·Set·Learn

The Shape of Things

Directions: Solve the problems in the shapes. Can you name each shape? Color the shapes that you can identify.

1.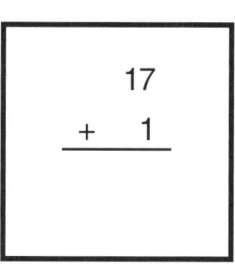
   17
   + 1

2. 24
   + 41

3. 72
   + 11

4.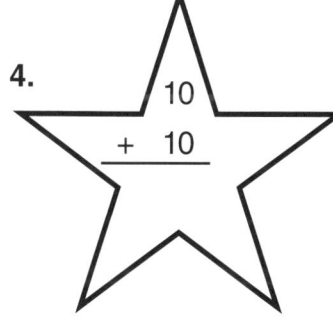
   10
   + 10

5. 25
   + 31
   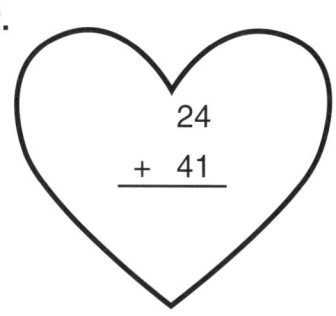

6.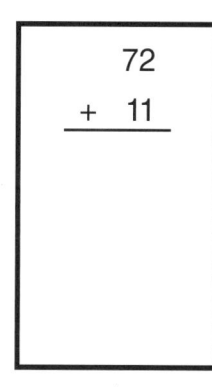
   19
   + 40

7.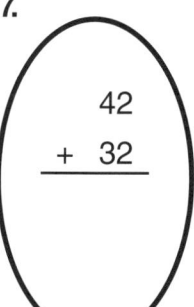
   42
   + 32

8. 81
   + 11
   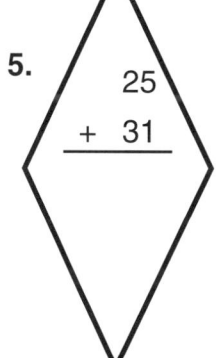

9. 20
   + 40
   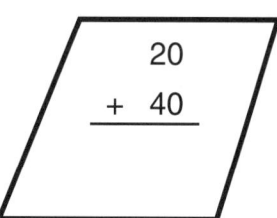

10. 12
    + 35
    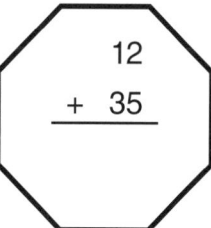

©Teacher Created Resources   21   #5939 Addition

What Is It?

Directions: To discover the secret shape below, follow the directions. Find the sums. Then connect the answers with a line. Connect the first answer with the second answer and the second answer with the third answer. Continue until you finish the shape.

1.   17
   + 22

2.   54
   + 21

3.   76
   + 22

4.   18
   + 31

5.   70
   + 20

6.   11
   + 11

7.   51
   + 27

8.   19
   + 10

9.   62
   + 22

10. 35
   + 21

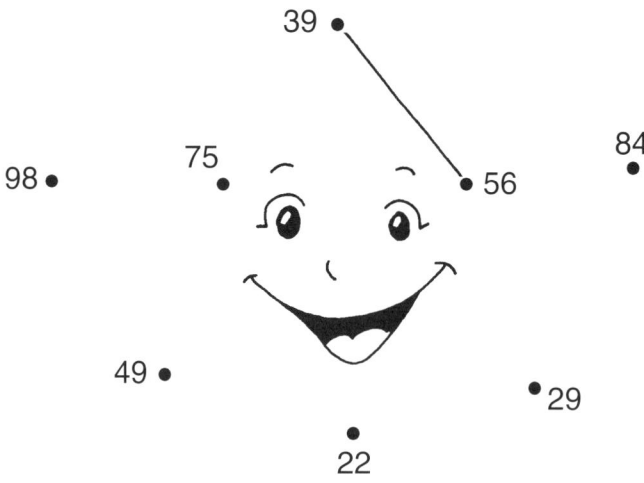

Secret Number

Directions: To discover the secret number, find the sums and follow the directions below.

1.	2.	3.
21 + 18	31 + 16	31 + 21
4.	5.	6.
41 + 31	12 + 12	10 + 17

- It is not number 24. Cross it out.
- It is not number 39. Cross it out.
- It is not number 52. Cross it out.
- It is not number 72. Cross it out.
- It is not number 47. Cross it out.

What is the secret number? _____

Add and Color

Directions: Find the sums. Then follow the directions and color the picture.

- Use a red crayon to color blocks with sums of 24.
- Use a yellow crayon to color blocks with sums of 38.
- Use a blue crayon to color blocks with sums of 41.
- Use a green crayon to color blocks with sums of 57.

1. 20 + 21	2. 26 + 12	3. 12 + 12
4. 32 + 25	5. 14 + 10	6. 15 + 42
7. 11 + 13	8. 15 + 23	9. 11 + 30

Add and Draw

Directions: Guess what is in the box. Find the sums. Then write the letter in each box that matches each sum. Read the word you spell and draw it in the box.

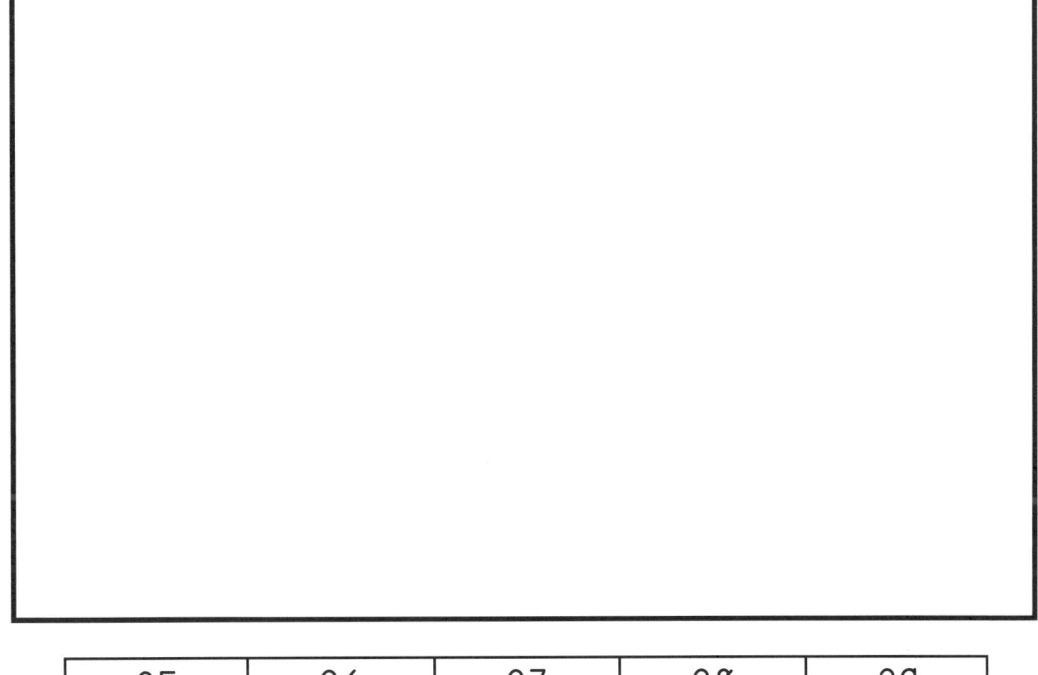

25	26	27	28	29
k	c	a	o	l

```
 13      14    11    16    13    12
+14     +12   +18   +12   +13   +13
———     ———   ———   ———   ———   ———
 27
  a
```

Hop to It

Directions: Find each sum.

1. 2 + 18 = ☐

2. 4 + 19 = ☐

3. 14 + 22 = ☐

4. 17 + 5 = ☐

5. 8 + 12 = ☐

6. 16 + 23 = ☐

7. 11 + 6 = ☐

8. 15 + 17 = ☐

9. 21 + 19 = ☐

10. 13 + 24 = ☐

Sailing into Addition

Directions: What a great day to go sailing! Solve the problems on each sail. Write the answers on the boats.

1. 10 + 67 =
2. 44 + 22 =
3. 32 + 47 =
4. 61 + 28 =
5. 85 + 14 =
6. 73 + 16 =
7. 24 + 35 =

Secret Message

Directions: To discover the secret message below, find the sums. Then place each letter in the matching numbered space.

A.	B.	C.	D.	E.	G.
20	23	51	15	10	26
+ 22	+ 12	+ 10	+ 14	+ 10	+ 11

I.	L.	M.	N.	O.	R.
31	42	51	53	24	21
+ 20	+ 11	+ 41	+ 31	+ 43	+ 10

S.	T.	U.	W.	Y.
33	13	24	34	62
+ 33	+ 12	+ 15	+ 14	+ 10

___ ___ ___ ___ ___ ___ ___ ___ ___ ___ ___ ___ ___ ___ !
61 67 84 37 31 42 25 39 53 42 25 51 67 84 66

___ ___ ___ ___ ___ ___ ___ ___ ___ ___ ___
72 67 39   42 31 20   42 29 29 51 84 37

___ ___ ___ ___ ___ ___ ___ ___ ___
25 48 67   29 51 37 51 25

___ ___ ___ ___ ___ ___ ___ .
84 39 92 35 20 31 66

#5939 Addition   28   ©Teacher Created Resources

Fill in the Bubble

1. $\begin{array}{r} 5 \\ +\ 3 \\ \hline \end{array}$	Ⓐ 53 Ⓑ 8 Ⓒ 9 Ⓓ 2	**6.** $1 + 6 + 2 =$ Ⓐ 7 Ⓑ 10 Ⓒ 12 Ⓓ 9
2. $\begin{array}{r} 41 \\ +\ 12 \\ \hline \end{array}$	Ⓐ 18 Ⓑ 8 Ⓒ 15 Ⓓ 53	**7.** $6 + 3 + 0 =$ Ⓐ 9 Ⓑ 8 Ⓒ 6 Ⓓ 63
3. $3 + 3 + 2 =$	Ⓐ 9 Ⓑ 18 Ⓒ 80 Ⓓ 8	**8.** $\begin{array}{r} 42 \\ +\ 3 \\ \hline \end{array}$ Ⓐ 45 Ⓑ 52 Ⓒ 40 Ⓓ 67
4. $\begin{array}{r} 42 \\ +\ 22 \\ \hline \end{array}$	Ⓐ 22 Ⓑ 60 Ⓒ 64 Ⓓ 20	**9.** $\begin{array}{r} 35 \\ +\ 2 \\ \hline \end{array}$ Ⓐ 77 Ⓑ 17 Ⓒ 37 Ⓓ 73
5. $\begin{array}{r} 3 \\ 4 \\ +\ 2 \\ \hline \end{array}$	Ⓐ 9 Ⓑ 12 Ⓒ 11 Ⓓ 7	**10.** $\begin{array}{r} 53 \\ +\ 45 \\ \hline \end{array}$ Ⓐ 8 Ⓑ 98 Ⓒ 18 Ⓓ 89

Regroup for Addition

Directions: Add each problem. Write how many tens. Write how many ones.

	Tens	Ones
1. 7 + 9 = ☐		
2. 4 + 7 = ☐		
3. 3 + 8 = ☐		
4. 9 + 5 = ☐		
5. 6 + 6 = ☐		

Directions: Fill in the missing numbers.

6. 17 is made up of ☐ ten and ☐ ones.

7. 12 is made up of ☐ ten and ☐ ones.

8. 14 is made up of ☐ ten and ☐ ones.

More Regrouping

Directions: When adding two digits, always start on the ones side first.

1. tens | ones
    39
    + 13

2. tens | ones
    42
    + 28

3. tens | ones
    61
    + 19

4. tens | ones
    25
    + 25

5. tens | ones
    36
    + 36

6. tens | ones
    18
    + 17

Double the Fun

Directions: Add each line of two-digit numbers.

1. 30
   + 12

2. 18
   + 16

3. 20
   + 10

4. 46
   + 30

5. 27
   + 34

6. 48
   + 42

7. 17
   + 22

8. 16
   + 12

9. 53
   + 37

10. Katherine has 12 toys. Her brother Braden has 11 toys. How many toys do they have altogether?

Addition in Space

Directions: Cross out each answer in the circle as you solve the problems.

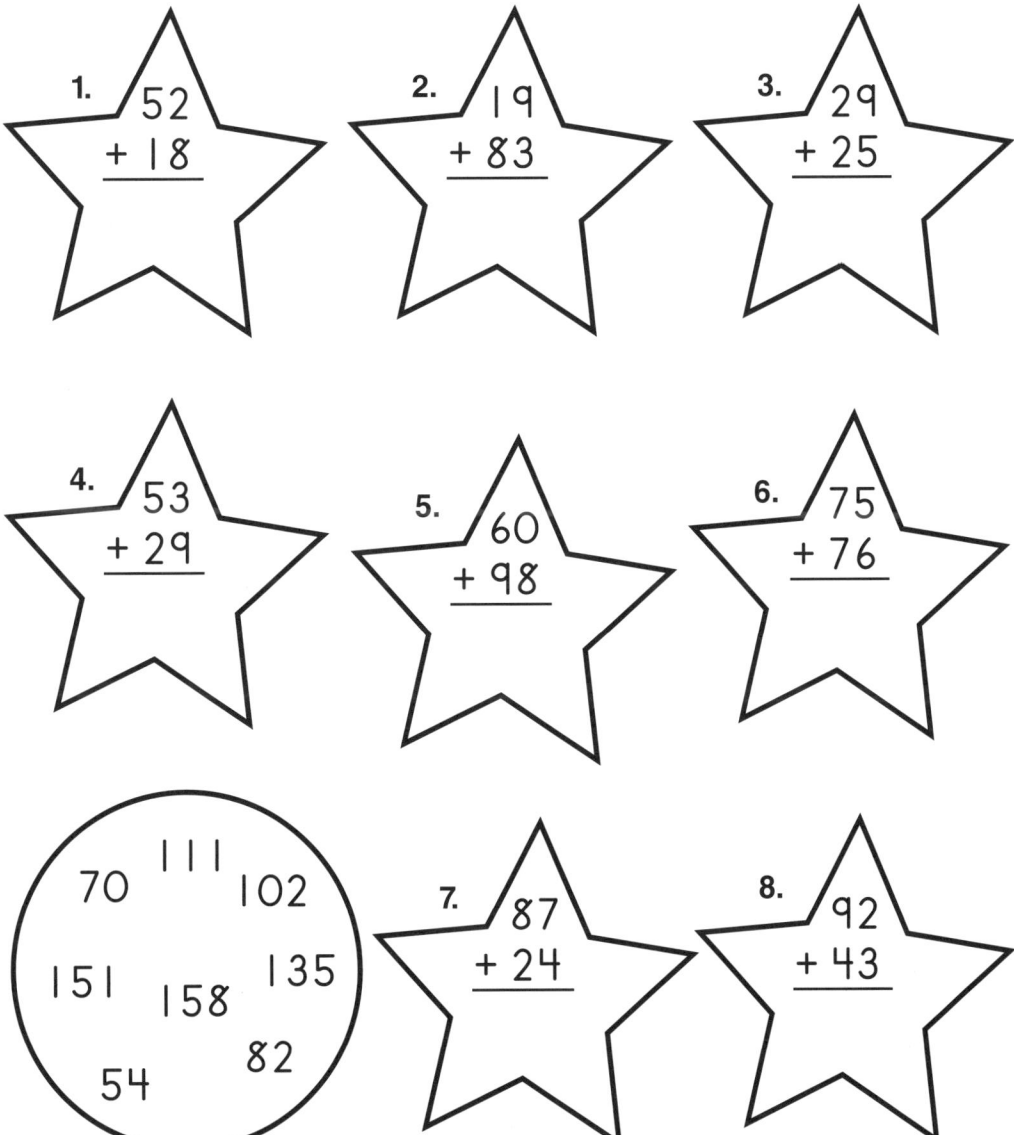

Mystery Animal

Directions: Guess what is in the box. Find the sums. Then write the letter in each box that matches each sum. Read the word you spell and draw it in the box.

48	49	50	51	52	53
s	e	a	o	h	r

```
  23        26      14      39      27      30
 +27       +26     +37     +14     +21     +19
 ---       ---     ---     ---     ---     ---
  50
```

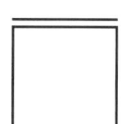
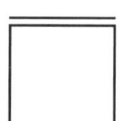
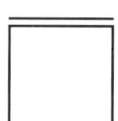
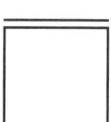

Another Mystery Animal

Directions: Guess what is in the box. Find the sums. Then write the letter in each box that matches each sum. Read the word you spell and draw it in the box.

80	81	82	83	84	85	86	87
d	e	a	o	c	r	l	i

45	24	62	58	12
+37	+60	+23	+25	+72

82

36	40	52	32	48
+47	+40	+35	+54	+33

 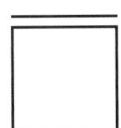 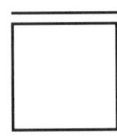 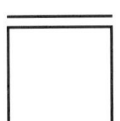 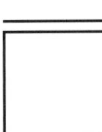

On Target

Directions: Find the sums of the numbers on the target. Where did Aaron's arrow land if he hit 60? Color that ring green. Color the other rings that have even sums red. Color the rings that have odd sums yellow.

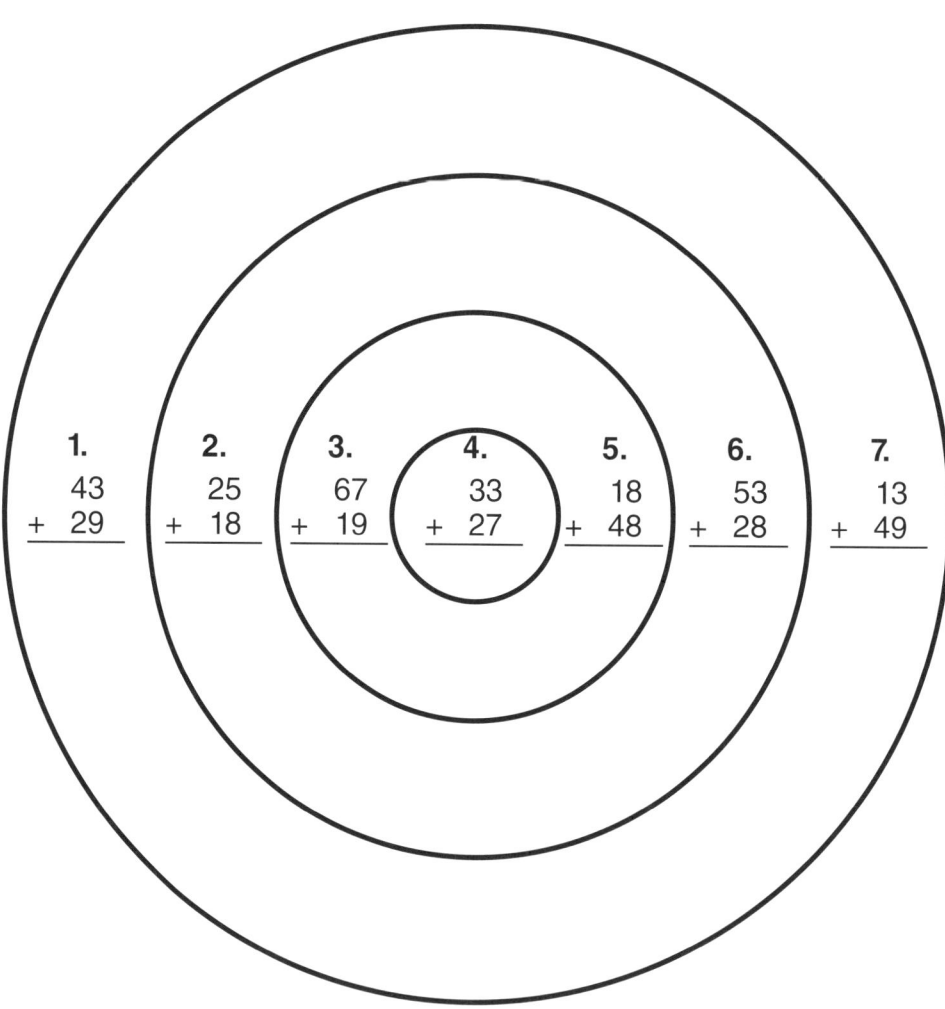

Hidden Treasure

Directions: Solve the problems by adding.

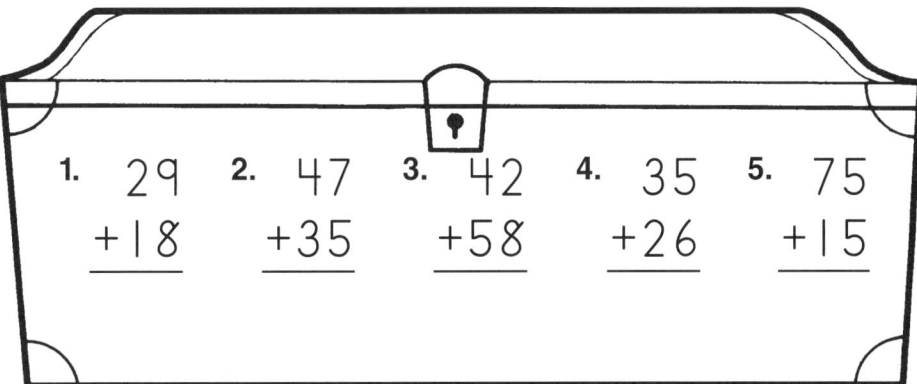

1. 29 +18
2. 47 +35
3. 42 +58
4. 35 +26
5. 75 +15

6. 32 +29
7. 43 +68
8. 43 +38
9. 74 +18
10. 27 +17

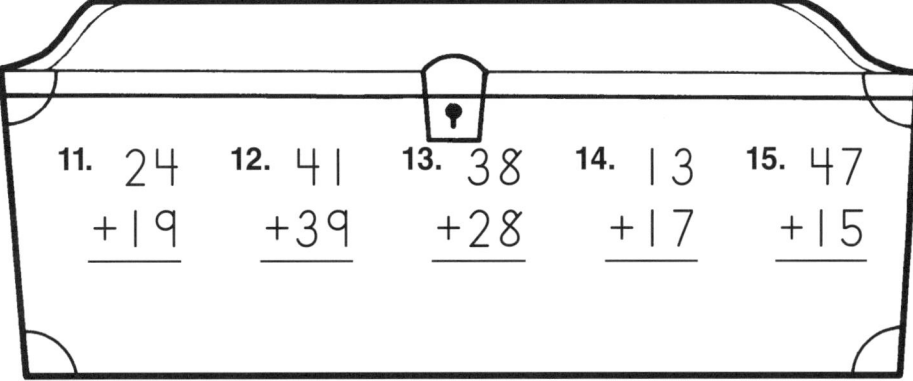

11. 24 +19
12. 41 +39
13. 38 +28
14. 13 +17
15. 47 +15

Adding Practice

Directions: Find the sums.

1. $\begin{array}{r}29\\+48\\\hline\end{array}$	2. $\begin{array}{r}14\\+75\\\hline\end{array}$	3. $\begin{array}{r}74\\+68\\\hline\end{array}$	4. $\begin{array}{r}97\\+50\\\hline\end{array}$
5. $\begin{array}{r}37\\+95\\\hline\end{array}$	6. $\begin{array}{r}20\\+52\\\hline\end{array}$	7. $\begin{array}{r}38\\+15\\\hline\end{array}$	8. $\begin{array}{r}45\\+29\\\hline\end{array}$
9. $\begin{array}{r}10\\+36\\\hline\end{array}$	10. $\begin{array}{r}41\\+52\\\hline\end{array}$	11. $\begin{array}{r}25\\+49\\\hline\end{array}$	12. $\begin{array}{r}34\\+17\\\hline\end{array}$
13. $\begin{array}{r}56\\+26\\\hline\end{array}$	14. $\begin{array}{r}27\\+30\\\hline\end{array}$	15. $\begin{array}{r}39\\+27\\\hline\end{array}$	16. $\begin{array}{r}74\\+19\\\hline\end{array}$

Ready·Set·Learn

More Adding Practice

Directions: Find the sums.

1. $\begin{array}{r} 11 \\ + 50 \\ \hline \end{array}$	2. $\begin{array}{r} 69 \\ + 12 \\ \hline \end{array}$	3. $\begin{array}{r} 69 \\ + 16 \\ \hline \end{array}$	4. $\begin{array}{r} 36 \\ + 13 \\ \hline \end{array}$
5. $\begin{array}{r} 64 \\ + 42 \\ \hline \end{array}$	6. $\begin{array}{r} 72 \\ + 38 \\ \hline \end{array}$	7. $\begin{array}{r} 71 \\ + 59 \\ \hline \end{array}$	8. $\begin{array}{r} 29 \\ + 80 \\ \hline \end{array}$
9. $\begin{array}{r} 24 \\ + 93 \\ \hline \end{array}$	10. $\begin{array}{r} 48 \\ + 18 \\ \hline \end{array}$	11. $\begin{array}{r} 13 \\ + 68 \\ \hline \end{array}$	12. $\begin{array}{r} 51 \\ + 17 \\ \hline \end{array}$
13. $\begin{array}{r} 17 \\ + 20 \\ \hline \end{array}$	14. $\begin{array}{r} 52 \\ + 11 \\ \hline \end{array}$	15. $\begin{array}{r} 41 \\ + 96 \\ \hline \end{array}$	16. $\begin{array}{r} 19 \\ + 91 \\ \hline \end{array}$

Let's Go Shopping!

Directions: Use the prices in the box to write addition problems below. Find the sums.

1. 🧥 + 👟 =

   ____ + ____ = ____

2. 👖 + 👟 =

   ____ + ____ = ____

3. 👗 + 👖 =

   ____ + ____ = ____

4. ⌚ + 🎩 =

   ____ + ____ = ____

Pick a Hat

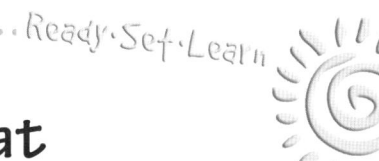

Directions: Find each sum. Draw a circle around the hat with the smallest sum.

1.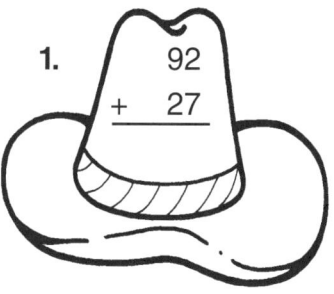
   92 + 27

2.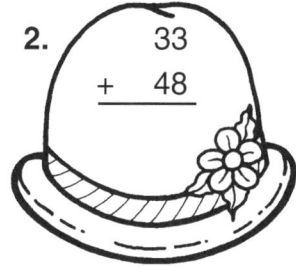
   33 + 48

3.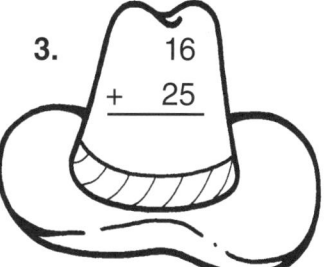
   16 + 25

4.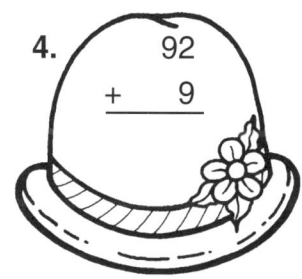
   92 + 9

5.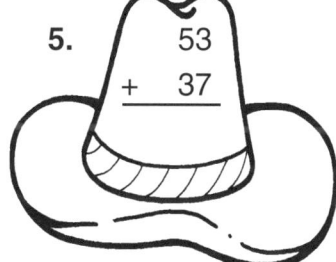
   53 + 37

6.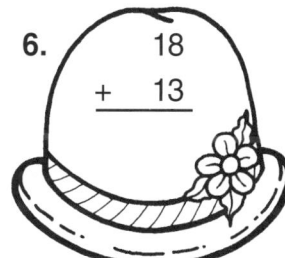
   18 + 13

7.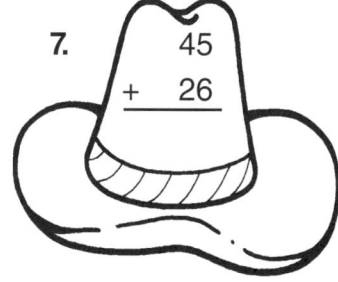
   45 + 26

8.
   75 + 27

9.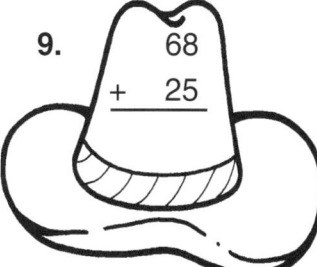
   68 + 25

Foxy Addition

Directions: Help the fox find his den. Solve the problems. Draw a line from the fox to the den with the sum of 82. Color the fox.

1. 44
   + 37

2. 68
   + 12

3. 55
   + 33

4. 47
   + 35

5. 19
   + 70

6. 65
   + 24

Lightning Quick

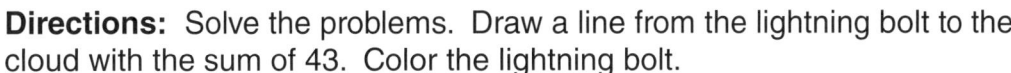

Directions: Solve the problems. Draw a line from the lightning bolt to the cloud with the sum of 43. Color the lightning bolt.

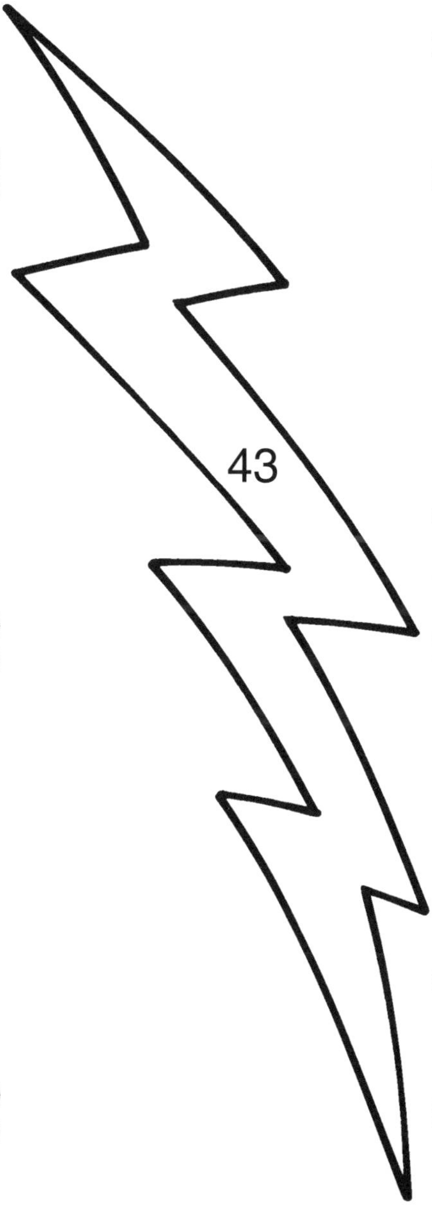

1. 32 + 13

2. 16 + 24

43

3. 27 + 12

4. 34 + 14

5. 26 + 13

6. 15 + 28

Read the Chart

Directions: Add these sums.

1. 87 + 9	2. 33 + 17	3. 64 + 26	4. 13 + 49	5. 25 + 25

Directions: Use the chart to answer the questions. Fill in the correct circle.

Player	Friday	Saturday
Benita	54	26
Ken	68	14
Forest	36	48

6. What was the total number of points scored by Forest?

    78   76   84
    ○   ○   ○

7. What was the total number of points scored by Ken?

    72   82   92
    ○   ○   ○

8. What was the total number of points scored by Benita?

    70   80   90
    ○   ○   ○

Zoo Math

Directions: Read each word problem. Write the math problem and solve.

1. At the zoo, Alicia fed the monkey 29 bananas and the elephant 47 peanuts. How many things did the animals eat in all?

   The animals ate _____ things in all.

   $$\begin{array}{r} 2\,9 \\ +\ 4\,7 \\ \hline \end{array}$$

2. Robbie watched the zookeeper feed the seals. The first seal ate 12 fish. The second seal ate 27 fish. How many fish did the seals eat in all?

   The seals ate _____ fish in all.

3. The flamingos love to eat shrimp. The flamingos ate 25 shrimp in the morning and 19 shrimp in the afternoon. How many shrimp did the flamingos eat in one day?

   The flamingos ate _____ shrimp in one day.

4. There were 67 kids in the petting zoo. Then 30 more kids came and joined them. How many kids are now in the petting zoo?

   There are _____ kids in the petting zoo.

5. Write your own word problem.

   _____
   _____
   _____
   _____

Keep the Change

Directions: Add the total amount.

1. + +  = _____

2.  +  + = _____

3.  + = _____

4. + + = _____

5.  +  = _____

Draw the coins to solve the following problem:

6. Tristan has two quarters, one dime, and one nickel. How much money does he have?

_____

Purchase, Please

Directions: Circle the coins to show the price of each item.

1.  76 cents

2.  47 cents

3.  30 cents

4.  75 cents

5. Marcie wants to buy a toy that costs 50 cents. Draw the coins she would need.

Window Shopping

Directions: Shade the square that shows the correct amount of coins needed to buy the treat listed.

1. The amount needed for the cupcake:

    24¢

    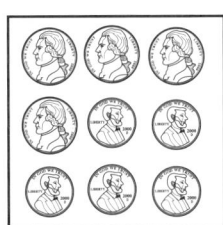

2. The amount needed for the donut:

    55¢

   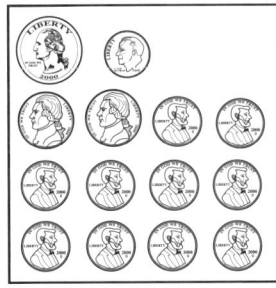 

3. The amount needed for the dozen chocolate chip cookies:

   75¢

4. Look at the cinnamon roll.
   Which coins would you need to buy one?

   How many dimes? _____

   How many nickels? _____

   67¢   How many pennies? _____

How Much Money?

Directions: Add the coins. Write the amount. Include the correct money symbol in your answer.

1. _____

2. _____

3. _____

4. _____

5. _____

How Many?

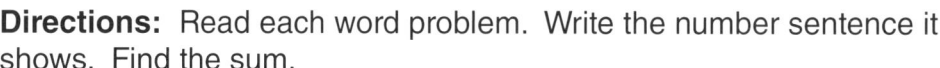

Directions: Read each word problem. Write the number sentence it shows. Find the sum.

1.

   In the forest, Lisa counted 53 pine trees, 24 spider webs, and 12 chipmunks. How many things did she count in all?

2.

   In Bill's classroom there are 57 pencils, 24 pieces of chalk, and 43 bottles of glue. How many supplies are there in all?

3.

   At the park, Carla counted 24 ducks, 32 children, and 34 roller skates. How many things did she count in all?

4.

   James counted 36 stars one night, 40 stars the next, and 67 stars on the third night. How many stars did he count in all?

Adding Three Numbers

Directions: Find the sums.

1.
```
   39
   57
+  47
```

2.
```
   39
   12
+  72
```

3.
```
   26
   71
+  59
```

4.
```
   17
   79
+  54
```

5.
```
   33
   75
+  23
```

6.
```
   51
   24
+  88
```

7.
```
   52
   30
+  18
```

8.
```
   39
   95
+  48
```

9.
```
   21
   53
+  17
```

10.
```
   42
   84
+  19
```

11.
```
   13
   38
+  42
```

12.
```
   27
   77
+  70
```

13.
```
   42
   26
+  49
```

14.
```
   23
   14
+  92
```

15.
```
   52
   38
+  14
```

16.
```
   59
   44
+  16
```

Three-Digit Addition

Directions: Write the answer to each addition problem.

1. 286 + 129 = 415

2. 297 + 302 =

3. 425 + 138 =

4. 507 + 126 =

5. 800 + 103 =

6. 727 + 163 =

7. 391 + 287 =

8. 215 + 609 =

9. 311 + 189 =

Practice Your Addition

Ready·Set·Learn

Directions: Fill in the bubble next to each correct answer.

1. 16 + 25	Ⓐ 9 Ⓑ 41 Ⓒ 40 Ⓓ 21	7. 42 + 28 =	Ⓐ 16 Ⓑ 60 Ⓒ 70 Ⓓ 72
2. 17 + 4	Ⓐ 13 Ⓑ 10 Ⓒ 21 Ⓓ 9	8. 123 + 797	Ⓐ 820 Ⓑ 810 Ⓒ 910 Ⓓ 920
3. 15 + 26	Ⓐ 31 Ⓑ 38 Ⓒ 41 Ⓓ 12	9. 15 + 7 + 3	Ⓐ 35 Ⓑ 33 Ⓒ 25 Ⓓ 26
4. 37 + 6 =	Ⓐ 31 Ⓑ 43 Ⓒ 42 Ⓓ 76	10. 202 + 505	Ⓐ 507 Ⓑ 717 Ⓒ 707 Ⓓ 705
5. 87 + 45	Ⓐ 132 Ⓑ 122 Ⓒ 120 Ⓓ 142	11. 90 + 60	Ⓐ 30 Ⓑ 96 Ⓒ 130 Ⓓ 150
6. 47 + 35 + 5	Ⓐ 77 Ⓑ 83 Ⓒ 87 Ⓓ 97	12. 94 + 57	Ⓐ 151 Ⓑ 197 Ⓒ 141 Ⓓ 179

Triple the Fun

Directions: Find each sum.

1. 675 + 321

2. 851 + 123

3. 729 + 148

4. 235 + 102

5. 463 + 333

6. 581 + 401

7. 134 + 100

8. 102 + 101

9. 900 + 100

Directions: Now it's your turn! In the space below, create three addition problems of your own. Remember, each number should have three digits.

10.   + _____

11.   + _____

12.   + _____

Practice, Practice, Practice

Directions: Practice your addition by adding these three-digit numbers.

1. 444 + 132	2. 821 + 123	3. 321 + 231
4. 555 + 264	5. 871 + 112	6. 899 + 100
7. 789 + 100	8. 412 + 402	9. 222 + 444

Directions: Solve each addition problem.

10. Cassidy has 123 pennies. Her friend Todd has 112 pennies. How many pennies do they have altogether?

    _____ + _____ = _____

11. Last summer Ruth and Ruby planted 112 flowers. This summer their friends Pat and Ann helped them plant 121 more. How many flowers do they have now?

    _____ + _____ = _____

Addition Magician

Directions: Add to find the sum.

1. 115 + 113

2. 204 + 164

3. 148 + 152

4. 407 + 51

5. 91 + 116

6. 112 + 257

7. 99 + 120

8. 224 + 325

9. 313 + 133

Dazzling Addition

Directions: Add each problem to find the answer.

1.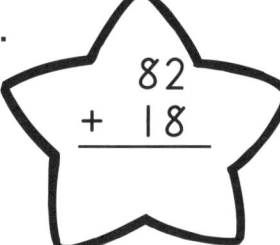
   82
   + 18

2. 34
   + 76

3.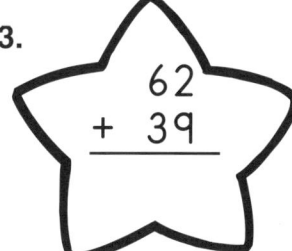
   62
   + 39

4.
   15
   +117

5. 18
   + 94

6.
   21
   +189

7.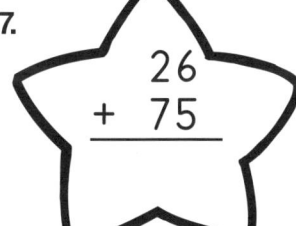
   26
   + 75

8. 83
   + 47

9.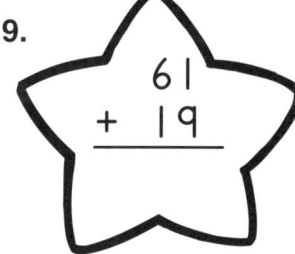
   61
   + 19

10.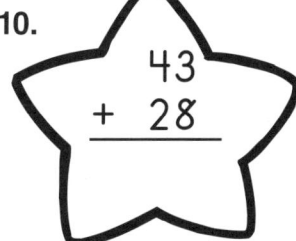
    43
    + 28

11. 44
    + 67

12.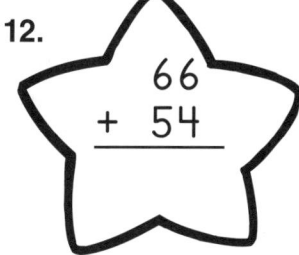
    66
    + 54

Mixed-Up Math

1. Six students in Mrs. Mann's class each used the stapler three times during the day. How many times was the stapler used?

   _____ times

2. Solve this problem. Write your answer in the box.

   34 + 54 = ☐

3. Solve the problem. Write your answer on the line.

   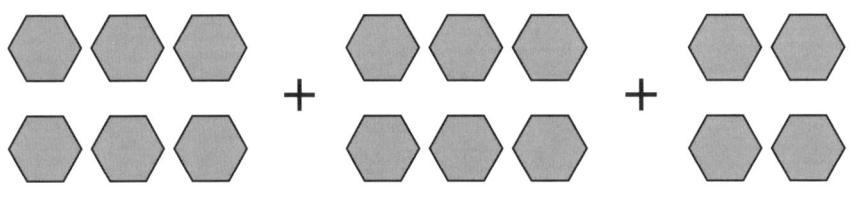

   _____

4. Jason earned 342 points playing a video game. That night, he scored another 234 points. How many total points did Jason earn playing the video game?

   _____ points

More Mixed-Up Math

1. Kurt played soccer for 43 minutes before school and 28 minutes after school. How many total minutes did Kurt play soccer?

   _____ minutes

2. Deron raises cows. Twenty-eight of the cows are white with spots. Twenty-five are all black. How many cows does Deron have in his herd?

   _____ cows

3. Tracy bought a book yesterday. She has already read 45 pages. She needs to read 37 more pages to finish the book. How many pages does the book have?

   _____ pages

4. Jennifer has 12 purple shirts. Liz has 8 more purple shirts than Jennifer. How many purple shirts do the two girls have in all?

   _____ purple shirts

Answer Key

Page 4
1. 7
2. 10
3. 17
4. 14
5. 14

Page 5
1. 2
2. 3
3. 1
4. 0
5. 4
6. 6
7. 8
8. 5
9. 9

Page 6
1. 8
2. 10
3. 14
4. 11
5. 12
6. 12

Page 7
1. 2, orange
2. 0, green
3. 4, red
4. 3, purple

Page 8
1. 16
2. 14
3. 14
4. 15
5. 12
6. 15
7. 17
8. 18
9. 16
10. 15
11. 18
12. 17
13. 3
14. 10
15. 6
16. 12

Page 9
1. 18
2. 18
3. 17
4. 17
5. 14
6. 14
7. 15
8. 15
9. 12
10. 12

Page 10
1. 10
2. 14
3. 18
4. 4
5. 12
6. 6
7. 2
8. 8
9. 16
10. 20
11. 10

Page 11
1. 15
2. 14
3. 9
4. 6
5. 13
6. 14
7. 15
8. 15
9. 9
10. 3
11. 2
12. 4

Page 12
1. 2
2. 3
3. 16
4. 17
5. 14
6. 15
7. 10
8. 11
9. 6
10. 7
11. 18
12. 19
13. 8
14. 9
15. 4
16. 5
17. 12
18. 13

Page 13
1. 9, 17
2. 12, 18
3. 10, 15
4. 8, 15
5. 6, 15
6. 7, 8
7. 11, 16
8. 8, 12
9. 14, 17
10. 3
11. 4
12. 0

Page 14
Row 1: 13, 10, 12, 11
Row 2: 17, 8, 10, 15
Row 3: 9, 19, 16, 8

Page 15
1. 12
2. 10
3. 11
4. 8
5. 6
6. 7
7. 9

Page 16
1. 12
2. 7
3. 14
4. 10
5. 9
6. 9
7. 11
8. 8
9. 11
10. 8
11. 10
12. 13

Page 17
1. $9 + $5 = $14
2. $9 + $3 = $12
3. $7 + $2 = $9
4. $5 + $1 + $2 = $8
5. $4 + $9 = $13
6. $7 + $5 = $12

Page 18
1. 3 + 4 + 6 = 13
2. 7 + 8 + 1 = 16
3. 6 + 5 + 9 = 20
4. 3 + 5 + 6 = 14

Page 19
1. 66
2. 99
3. 60
4. 87
5. 58
6. 98
7. 92
8. 49
9. 86
10. 88
11. 38
12. 89
13. 38, 49, 58, 60, 66, 86, 87, 88, 89, 92, 98, 99

Page 20
1. 33
2. 29
3. 64
4. 29
5. 34
6. 62
7. 43
8. 53
9. 59

Page 21
1. 18
2. 65
3. 83
4. 20
5. 56
6. 59
7. 74
8. 92
9. 60
10. 47

Answer Key (cont.)

Page 22
1. 39
2. 75
3. 98
4. 49
5. 90
6. 22
7. 78
8. 29
9. 84
10. 56

Page 23
1. 39
2. 47
3. 52
4. 72
5. 24
6. 27

The secret number is 27.

Page 24
1. 41
2. 38
3. 24
4. 57
5. 24
6. 57
7. 24
8. 38
9. 41

Page 25
27, 26, 29, 28, 26, 25 = a clock

Page 26
1. 20
2. 23
3. 36
4. 22
5. 20
6. 39
7. 17
8. 32
9. 40
10. 37

Page 27
1. 77
2. 66
3. 79
4. 89
5. 99
6. 89
7. 59

Page 28
A. 42
B. 35
C. 61
D. 29
E. 20
G. 37
I. 51
L. 53
M. 92
N. 84
O. 67
R. 31
S. 66
T. 25
U. 39
W. 48
Y. 72

Secret Message: Congratulations! You are adding two-digit numbers.

Page 29
1. B
2. D
3. D
4. C
5. A
6. D
7. A
8. A
9. C
10. B

Page 30
1. 16, 1, 6
2. 11, 1, 1
3. 11, 1, 1
4. 14, 1, 4
5. 12, 1, 2
6. 1, 7
7. 1, 2
8. 1, 4

Page 31
1. 52
2. 70
3. 80
4. 50
5. 72
6. 35

Page 32
1. 42
2. 34
3. 30
4. 76
5. 61
6. 90
7. 39
8. 28
9. 90
10. 23

Page 33
1. 70
2. 102
3. 54
4. 82
5. 158
6. 151
7. 111
8. 135

Page 34
50, 52, 51, 53, 48, 49 = a horse

Page 35
82, 84, 85, 83, 84, 83, 80, 87, 86, 81 = a crocodile

Page 36
1. 72
2. 43
3. 86
4. 60
5. 66
6. 81
7. 62

Page 37
1. 47
2. 82
3. 100
4. 61
5. 90
6. 61
7. 111
8. 81
9. 92
10. 44
11. 43
12. 80
13. 66
14. 30
15. 62

Page 38
1. 77
2. 89
3. 142
4. 147
5. 132
6. 72
7. 53
8. 74
9. 46
10. 93
11. 74
12. 51
13. 82
14. 57
15. 66
16. 93

Page 39
1. 61
2. 81
3. 85
4. 49
5. 106
6. 110
7. 130
8. 109
9. 117
10. 66
11. 81
12. 68
13. 37
14. 63

Answer Key (cont.)

Page 39 (cont.)
15. 137
16. 110

Page 40
1. $49 + $57 = $106
2. $32 + $57 = $89
3. $26 + $32 = $58
4. $64 + $17 = $81

Page 41
1. 119
2. 81
3. 41
4. 101
5. 90
6. 31
7. 71
8. 102
9. 93

Page 42
1. 81
2. 80
3. 88
4. 82
5. 89
6. 89

Page 43
1. 45
2. 40
3. 39
4. 48
5. 39
6. 43

Page 44
1. 96
2. 50
3. 90
4. 62
5. 50
6. 84
7. 82
8. 80

Page 45
1. 76
2. 39
3. 44
4. 97

Page 46
1. 31¢
2. 60¢
3. 24¢
4. 16¢
5. 80¢
6. 65¢

Page 47
Some problems have more than one solution.
1. 3 quarters, 1 penny
2. 2 dimes, 5 nickels, 2 pennies
3. 1 quarter, 1 nickel
4. 2 quarters, 5 nickels
5. any combination of coins equaling 50¢

Page 48
1. 1st square
2. 1st square
3. 2nd square
4. 6 dimes, 1 nickel, 2 pennies

Page 49
1. 70¢
2. 67¢
3. 56¢
4. $1.00
5. 77¢

Page 50
1. 53 + 24 + 12 = 89
2. 57 + 24 + 43 = 124
3. 24 + 32 + 34 = 90
4. 36 + 40 + 67 = 143

Page 51
1. 143
2. 123
3. 156
4. 150
5. 131
6. 163
7. 100
8. 182
9. 91

10. 145
11. 93
12. 174
13. 117
14. 129
15. 104
16. 119

Page 52
1. 415
2. 599
3. 563
4. 633
5. 903
6. 890
7. 678
8. 824
9. 500

Page 53
1. B
2. C
3. C
4. B
5. A
6. C
7. C
8. D
9. C
10. C
11. D
12. A

Page 54
1. 996
2. 974
3. 877
4. 337
5. 796
6. 982
7. 234
8. 203
9. 1,000

Page 55
1. 576
2. 944
3. 552
4. 819
5. 983
6. 999

7. 889
8. 814
9. 666
10. 235
11. 233

Page 56
1. 228
2. 368
3. 300
4. 458
5. 207
6. 369
7. 219
8. 549
9. 446

Page 57
1. 100
2. 110
3. 101
4. 132
5. 112
6. 210
7. 101
8. 130
9. 80
10. 71
11. 111
12. 120

Page 58
1. 18
2. 88
3. 16
4. 576

Page 59
1. 71
2. 53
3. 82
4. 32 (12 + 20 = 32)

This Award Is Presented To

_____

for

★ Doing Your Best

★ Trying Hard

★ Not Giving Up

★ Making a
  Great Effort